When her father Major John Jarmain died in the
Battle of Normandy on June 26, 1944, Joanna
Weston was six years old. A book of Jarmain's
poetry was published in 1945 and Joanna read the
poems again and again over the years in an attempt
to know the man behind the words. More than six
decades later, her own book of poems gives us a
poignant portrait of her absent father and her own
war-marred childhood. A *Summer Father* moves
from the child's longing for a father, to the adult's
revulsion from war, to knowledge and, finally,
acceptance of death and grief.

A Summer Father

Joanna M. Weston

Frontenac House
Calgary, Alberta

Book and cover design: Epix Design Inc.
Cover photo: Frantisek Staud (www.phototravels.net)
Author photo: Phiil Walmsley

Library and Archives Canada Cataloguing in Publication
Weston, Joanna M., 1938-
        A summer father / Joanna M. Weston.
Poems.
ISBN 1-897181-05-1
        1. Fathers and daughters--Poetry. 2. World War, 1939-1945--
Poetry. I. Title.
PS8595.E75S93 2006   C811'.54   C2006-904582-8

We acknowledge the support of the Canada Council for the Arts which last year invested $20.3 million in writing and publishing throughout Canada. We also acknowledge the support of The Alberta Foundation for the Arts.

Printed and bound in Canada
Published by Frontenac House Ltd.
1138 Frontenac Avenue S.W.
Calgary, Alberta, T2T 1B6, Canada
Tel: 403-245-2491   Fax: 403-245-2380
editor@frontenachouse.com   www.frontenachouse.com

Dedicated to my father,
Major John William Fletcher Jarmain,
who died on June 26, 1944 in Normandy, France

Acknowledgements

All quotations used as epigraphs are from a
collection of John Jarmain's poetry, titled *POEMS*,
published by Collins, London, U.K. in 1945.
Permission to quote from his poems granted by
Janet Coward and the Oasis Salamander Trust.

With heartfelt thanks to the poets of the Internet
Writing Workshop, Sans Nom, and the Cedar
Creek Writers, who have listened and critiqued,
to Dave Margoshes for his sharp-eyed editorial
help, and to my husband, Robert, for his ongoing
support and presence.

Poems from *A Summer Father* have appeared in
the following publications: *Amethyst Review*;
Citizen 32; *James River Poetry Review*; *The Ontario
Poetry Society*; *Outreach Connection*; *Raw Nervz*;
Target; *Third Half*; and the *Victoria Literary Times*.
They have also been published in the anthologies
Listening with the ear of the heart and *Waging Peace*,
and have been featured on CBC's *Gallery*.

Contents

A Summer Father

Two Cemeteries

*St.Peter's, Muenster, Saskatchewan
and Ranville, Normandy*

regulated rows
of uniform tombstones
intone names and dates

Ranville is where my
father's war ended

> close my eyes
> and there are roses
> on each grave
> mown velvet grass
> over battledress and gun
> where fields lay plain chant
> beyond this battalion
> of cross, star and crescent

enclosure here at St. Peter's –
tranquility
in requiem of snow

memorials lie black
on white stone
contained by hedge
and ministry of wind
over royal priesthood

> yet do the brothers lie in Normandy
> on a hill of blazing canticles –
> soldiers there transfigured?

perhaps my father lies here
patriarch in this
garrison of Christendom

I, beneath this overcast
experience a D-Day sky
and lose a summer father
in a funeral
whose psalm
is wind and sand

The Child Who Died

My childhood's soul awoke this dying night
And walked the rooms I walk, that were her own;

green cot broken in my father's war
blue dress gift to an artillery gun
teddy bear squashed in an overseas grave

no one remembers the child
who died of sirens
and the whisper pulling silence

I died slowly, and watched it happen
each bomb, each plane, took a small piece
and wrote another letter of my name on the sky

each bursting house buried another limb
until I was gone, without lament
to search for my childhood self
and the father who died
but I cannot reclaim the dead

Trees

did he remember
the apple trees
and the willow
at the end of our garden?

did he remember
how his children
ran to touch and touch
silver-grey bark?

he is recorded
in one photo
with his son
framed by leaves
and fruit

Loss

Mother lost
the green glass brooch
Father gave me

dropped it
between apple tree and lavender
somewhere on the path
to becoming an emerald

I clipped grass with scissors
turned soft earth
found a knife patterned with fish
and a spoon engraved with leaves

she sketched patterns of bark
details of miniature:
        an ant on a grass stem
        a speed of red spiders
while I wept
the emptiness of green

Studio Portrait, 1942

two children
caught in a black and white
photograph

my brother in shorts
and Fair Isle sweater
and me in smocked dress

frozen eyes
and tight mouths

dare not smile

we might break
spill
onto the carpet

turn it red

Ignore the Past

But this burst house with smoking twisted stair,
These scattered limbs in fields of asphodel,

I prefer to avoid
the child watching bombs
empty out of the sky

I walk around her, ignore her
leave her standing
head back, mouth open

I will walk to the village store
and the siren will not wail
I will not feel earth vomit
brick, plaster
plumbing, grass, chairs, plates
and tattered flesh

the child's mouth is full
of broken houses
and her body
part of the lost green lawn

I walk on and do not see her
under the rubble of 1944

Starscapes

The crooked scorpion low across the South
Lies in the tent's small mouth
Like a curled and jewelled snake.

my brother and I set up
his African tent
under the Big Dipper
beside purple irises
and laburnum

we didn't see
the Southern Cross
beyond the tent flap
or grains of white sand
caught in the seams

A Nursery War

we played follow-the-spitfire
ring-a-ring-a-pilot-gone
the bomber's bridge has fallen down

here's one fair-lady-o
buried with no funeral
in the crook of a tree
hidden by blossom
so no one can find me

for I am the child
whose bones were ground
to make bread for war

Fingers on Glass

rain trying to come in
tapping entreaty
on the windowpane

I shrink from those cold fingers
and voices waiting
at the closed dark window

the eyes of downed pilots
war's bombed-out people
faces crushed and tear-marked

want me to let them
into my bedroom
I have no space for them

no room for their voices
and their tears
I am not old enough

and I press on the cold lens
lean against the pane
shouting "Go away. Go!"

my tears are like hands
with no one to hold them
tapping ... tapping on glass

An Old Dress

I cannot tell it now, the quickening touch,
The darkness melting into me like fire,

lift the lid of childhood
and I unpack Mother
shake her gently
take an iron to the creases
read jokes in the pleats
and poetry on the sleeves

fear has burnt the breast
grief been mended down the skirt
passion gathers at the waist
frivolity embroiders the hem

the dress hangs limply
I turn it on the hanger
and discover a day
spent rowing in dappled sunlight

an old dress, a tired dress
but wind lifts the skirt
and Father's hand is on her thigh

Soft Answers

between all the mornings
and "good nights"
lie questions
a child would ask
and a father answer

Like Other People's Fathers

Had he been hiding in all my childhood moods…?

would he open
the curtains
for his daughter
and let starlight in?

break the blackout?

catch bombs
before they fell?

Fidelity

Surely her words were written in loneliness

the antique lyric
behind her eyes
Mother threw on canvas
when no one was looking

touched its music into life
with thin layers of paint
and sang while night
closed arms on her body

she chanted dance out of dream
with grief under her skin
as my father slept
with foreign women

Through the Window

the brown curtain billowed
for planes to fly
into the room

leftover bombs
blew me out of my bed
blasted me through the window
out, with nowhere to hide
from the sound
of them coming
to take me as part
of their roar
across the shadowed sky

bed empty
my body gone
across a sky filled
with slivers of window frame
that pinned me to the planes
so that I would be
a bomb for them

my nodding dead body
dropped away
                           dropped
into the nothing dark

ack-ack shells
caught my falling
fired me back
back to stars beyond
the room with the curtain blowing
over emptiness

The Playing Field

church bazaars and Saturday football
happened on the playing field
sheltered between lines
of beech and oak

peopled with laughter
cheers and change
       behind them
       an ack-ack station
       held safety
       with upraised snout
       and night-time bullets

walking there
years later
I hear memory
spoken by my brother
who knew and could not
forget the sounds
that held him
rigid in his bed
while I plugged ears
and mind
against recollection

Let's Pretend

a battalion
marches
down the street

one soldier
peels away
step in step

opens the green gate
and strides the path
to our front door

Father had come home

until I read his name
on a tombstone
in France

Inheritance

he shows my brother
how to peel an orange

cutting the astringency of skin
into precise quarter sections
and curling each one
carefully away

my brother teaches me

I show my sons

and watch bright peel
bite the table's waxed surface

His Poems

Listen! These poems were not made in rooms,
But out in the empty sand,

open the book
and the words
are Father
reading bedtime stories
of war and
bombs and
fear to me, his daughter
who will not sleep
because there is no one
to leave the night-light on
no one to say "Sleep well"
before Spitfires fall
into this dream I have…

I go into the garden quickly
to see planes dodging
circling
         looping
                  diving
I shout at them
"Go away, or you will die"
and point my finger at one

it comes
lazily
        down
                the sky
thin smoke trailing behind

a parachute opens and comes
gently to my garden. I find
the pilot lying, watching
me. I point
at him and say "You are dead"

he is tangled in his harness, fingers
clutch chords, blood trails
over hands, face, jacket
helmet undone and askew

I bury him under the irises
by the laburnum tree

no one knows what I found
or did, that day

I go out and read
in the summer grass
to hear leaves shifting
my heart beating

I turn pages
and hear eyes closing
under the grass, fingers
pushing dandelions, warmth
bleeding into the ground

A Book Called "Poems"

They had no peace at their creation,
No twilight hush of wings;

sixty-four pages
worn and creased
with split binding
that travelled
from my childhood
to this present

his words lift
to thud in sunlit sand
and bloody shadows
as Father campaigns
to put gunfire and dead men
on paper

Embarkation

Only a few officials holding watches
Noted the stealthy hour of our departing,
And, as we went, turned back to their hotel.

the train moves slowly
from the station

Father goes without goodbye
into the soldier's comradeship
of linked solitudes

pistons heave, wheels draw them
down the track, out of dawn
to quayside and a somber song
that whispers and lifts
like smoke

war lies
ahead of the bow wave
beyond foam sliding past the ship's hull
beyond arcs of flying fish
out of sight
unimagined

Unknown

his shadow
moves on dark glass
with a voice
that commands
ruined cities
into poetry

Shield

how to shut out explosions

forget his children

find silence and shelter
between bombardments

to write poetry?

Midnight Soldiers

my words are ghostlier now, my breath unblessed

strangers who speak at midnight
of lanterns and women's laughter
tell me Father soldiered in Tunis
sailed to Sicily and Italy
then back across the Channel
leaving children
in bivouac towns

men recite the words he wrote
in ballads of wavering heat
where water is lazy mirage
nomads drink freely
and soldiers pant under fire

his poems go up and out
with the tramp of feet
across white deserts
to a land where kisses rise green
and his body holds the story

Aftermath

...Tobruk is now a name
And sacked and burned, like Troy.

Tobruk –
minarets
amongst gardens

the harbour fretted
by the leaning masts
and drowned hulls
of ancient battles

debris, decay
and a December poem
while another war
moves on
and warped ghosts
cry defeat

Blown Poems

We have seen sand frothing like the sea
About our wheels, and in our wake
Clouds rolling yellow and opaque,
Thick-smoking from the ground.

sand blows through his poems
hides the grey-faced men
who build roads
only to lose them
under storms

tornadoes of sand
take tents and soldiers
into the screaming sky

pass and leave silence

empty my father
who wrote in sand
waiting for wind
to carry the words

Parched

...should I walk toward that mocking lake
It would be ever far and ever seen,
Still unattained, still silver-clear and cold,

Moses' tribes would have
swallowed and seen
       taunting water

each thirst measured
stained tin
       by cracked lip

sip by urgent taste
between artillery and mirage –
an armed oasis

In Charge

Like shabby ghosts down dried-up river beds
The tired procession slowly leaves the field;
Dazed and abandoned, just a count of heads,

does the major envy
prisoners of war
their lost need to choose
as these phantoms of battle
file past
into a trammeled future?

or is each day
an order
handed down
to him
held captive
by command?

Items of Dress

the red cap
familiar
to the 51st
Highland Division
flowers
on his grave

the hazel stick
he carried
gives shade
to the cemetery

but his pipe smoke
curls
from another mouth

October, 1942

And there our dead will keep their holy ground.

El Alamein –
the place
where poetry
became need
beyond want

a way to put gunfire
bombs   minefields
sand drilling flesh
into order

a way to find respite
in a glimpse of magnolias –
moonlight on a sandbag wall

it was
the place of knowing
that only men who fought
at Alamein
would mark the map
with sand and yellow moon

we who come later
find lilies
and buried poems

Fragments

He sang for company as he shovelled the sand,
Digging himself a shelter for the night.

the desert gave him
hard sky over moving sand
instead of peacetime's
vineyards and summer sun

under the artillery of El Alamein
he found himself leached
by dunes and guns
alive by grace
from Tel-el-Eisa

here he viewed life
in small pictures –

a soldier
sang of orchids

wire twisted
a telephone pole
to crucifixion

a broken wall
for shelter –

poetry a luxury of time
when words slipped out
gritty and thin
exploding
sand and shrapnel
to portray
the inexplicable
to his daughter

On White Dunes

…a solitary ring plover,
Small and plump and coloured
– Black and white and red –
Surprising as a toy of painted wood.

between the ocean and the desert
a stray plover
from Scotland's Moray Firth
foraged on the dunes of El Alamein

it took him from rumbling tanks
and the smoking wrecks of jeeps
to where children played
under apple trees

Birdwatcher

...streams where the dipper haunts

the moonlit barn owl's
drift for prey

a springtime swirl of gulls
behind the plough

the kestrel's
hover into wind

seen through
hedges of memory
and bombardment

Keepsake

close the clasp
round a child's wrist

and the place
where Father chose a bracelet
for his daughter is held –

the smell of an Algerian bazaar
swirling under the cough of camels
as dung and incense
pervade foot-beaten streets
eddying through desert dialects
red brocade   blue carpet
and enamelled earrings

undo the clasp –
lay flat the filigreed rectangles of silver
painted faintly turquoise   pink and yellow

the dream spills
over my open hands
and nothing remains

Incongruities

...she that with her lover at her side
Is in her sleep impersonally destroyed,

how more can I find
this father
who worked his pen
in late night bivouac
and wrote the cruelty whereby
a lover bombs
other lovers
because the order is given
to make roses with fire?

how more is Father
written in my bones
exploding sentences
in my wartime dreams?

Sentinels

...with these silences I stand,
A shape of shadow in an empty place,

he drew a New Year line
between decades

watched a phantom sentry
move moonlight

across desert sand
with long fingers

and could not know
his daughter's shadow

Burial

I had my hair cut at Leptis Magna.
(That is the fact, the statement I wish to make.)

snippets fell on white sand
to be dragged away
by black ants
that raced hither and back
across his notebook
leaving trails
blind as gunfire

they took his hair down
to the buried city
built before Christ was born
of marble from Ferrara
paid for by scurrying Lepticans
then entombed by sand
and the industry of ants

Transient

And it had no thickness,
Like a large leaf painted on a teacup.

day's sibilants
whisper the street
in Alexandria
as a bat
touches my father
into a poem

a burnoused Arab
leans against a wall
where the moon lays
silver and shadow

the bat
with a wing-tip
breaches stillness
in this moment
stolen for privacy
before dawn
returns combat

Lost

his Sicilian poems
lie on a hillside

sheltered by an almond orchard
waiting for voices

to reach and live them
into D'Annunzian skies

those narrow roads
contain his words

a yellowhammer sings
from the hedge

and a poem flies
into my hands

Pictures

other places
where the major led
men into battle

Portopallo in sunshine
Vizzini coloured with flowers
Ramacca's angry farmsteads
Etna where he mailed a postcard
to his son

places of small
terraced houses
shell-torn and tangled
write their names
on photos men hold
of my father

but where are
the pictures
needed to paint him
for myself –
to put his final portrait
on paper of my own?

To Obliterate

he writes in his diary
around flecks of bombs
        that fall
making craters
where people shed flesh

he draws screams
over pages
where he has
erased names

D-Day

rain-laden sky hangs
over gray ocean and I know
this is not the last poem
my D-Day father lived
as he ran through waves
wrote words with pounding feet
and laid down lines of elegy
in gunfire

he shouted stanzas
to the stumbling brigade
verses stolen from the ship he'd left

clutched sonnets in his teeth
and spat them on the beaches
when the first soldiers fell

culled poems
from sliding sand
low cliffs and broken hedges

ballads to be sung
through coming years
to the drum of waves
where ghosts write
and tourists listen
to spectral poems
marching in the tide

The House Martin

Driving them to speed ...
Released like an arrow.
Then the fins become wings

bombs tremble
down the sky

swift as the skim of house martins
over a summer pond

air shakes and
dives Father to a ditch

he sees the flicker of the bird
black with white undersides

as it glides, darts over water
the bomb falls   the bird...

Said Alice

Robert Browning's poetry
Shakespeare
Alice in Wonderland

to these he stole
in the sudden quiet
between salvos

these his companions
in Africa
Sicily and France

but who spoke
in the last seconds?
whose voice
pulled him
down the rabbit hole?

did he hear
a child's voice
leading
to the dark?

Out and Down

Wait, and try not to hear.

Father threw his army boots
into the ditch
at Ste Honorine la Chardonnerette
and leapt with them
trying to follow Alice
down the rabbit hole

he discovered that Good Friday
happens in an explosive dawn
that stones roll over broken feet
hands clench on torn skull

he saw it all
as Alice turned her head

red cap, stick and pipe
he tossed after the boots
as he jumped from the jeep
to where the Red Queen
mocks the Mad Hatter

Happenstance

Where death remains and agony has been

that moment
when he died

an accident
of presence

when everything
except death
moved slowly

when he met
grass in a ditch
and shrapnel
found him

John Jarmain
June 26th
in Normandy

if I say
"He is dead"
often enough

if I say
"He was killed
on June 26, 1944"
often enough

it will be true
and I will
believe
Father is dead

but how many times
is enough?

and then... what if
the driver
had jumped
from the jeep?

what if
the major
had stayed?

would the story
be different?

To Touch

Only a worthless corpse of sense bereft,
Symbol of death, and sacrifice, and waste.

I rage through
Father's poems

tear pages to reach
through stanzas

try to grasp
the shadow between pages
rumours half-seen in a sonnet
in order to fill the space
his death detonated

I fume
at my father
who leapt
for a ditch

and died there

Absence

he is a voice
climbing sand dunes
quite unlike
the ones I walked
barefoot at Margate
without him

Afterwards

In you my whispered songs have met defeat

her man got lost beneath a French sky
mislaid under a falling bomb

Mother looked for him in newspapers
but found strangers in his uniform

discovered his bones under green turf
and painted them into his children

hung his eyes in their faces
and set his hands over theirs

she carved an archive of him
in the river where neighbours floated

armed and pointing at her
each mouth declaring lack of love

as pebbles fell like gunfire
and his portrait hung in a cave

drawn by a child
with blind hands and eyes

Grief

Mother hung his uniform
on the wall

undid the buttons
to taste goodbye

his children played
between the seams

The Storyteller

goldenrod tales flowed from her mouth
– sand in Africa, petals in Sicily –
as Mother breathed yellow flowers
into breast milk for children

recounting the stories
created under her brush
when the man she kissed
was buried under iris and lavender

Treasures

stained letters
on thin paper
written to Mother

the book of poetry
with his novel
on a bookshelf

faded photos
in an album
that my brother kept

the bracelet
I cannot yet give
to my granddaughter

Legacy

Father's face worn
by the grandson –
first of the family
to read his epitaph
in Normandy

Violent Poetry

... the smooth bright shapely shell
And the great gun lifted gleaming in the air,
Perfect with all the skill of men's contriving.

war was the longest poem
I ever lived:
words blew apart
in my mind
the letters settling
in torn ditches
flying through
broken windows
to rest
on tilted beds
or sliding down
un-walled floors

the epic writes itself
on barrage balloons
that fly across
night skies

war cemeteries
are stanzas carved
over red roses
while silent hands
point guns, bayonets
and I am pinioned
to a falling bomb
written into a ballad
that will cry
in another child

Army Next Door

I went looking
for the footprints
of my childhood war
under rhododendrons
and cedars

I found math exercises
tennis rackets, ribbons
old hockey scores
and smudged, pulped papers

      heard army voices shout
              amongst park trees
      troops deploy
      tanks crank past
      jeeps buzz destinations
      deserted forms drift
              like spring blossom
              into rubbished piles
      and I wondered why
      why we saved schoolbooks
      erased paragraphs
      "because of the war"

the soldiers vanished
 like Father
 in the space
 of one holiday
 left only a paved road
 around the park's perimeter
 which cracked, grew weeds
 disappeared

War Cemetery

I looked for
my father in a field
but found only
his name
out in public

I disliked
his being shared
by beetles, swallows
and the glazed view of tourists

wanted to erase his name
from eyes
wrapped around the letters
carrying them
all over the world
like ashes
on the wind

Normandy Beaches

Sifting the drifted sandhills grain by grain

his footprints lead
across the cliff
down to where
abandoned guns
straggle
on a beach

in my dream
I follow
the prints
>each one fainter
>than the last
>as sand
>trickles in
>to fill them

Grave

beside a yew tree
un cimetière militaire –
these peacetime roses

Finality

close the book

let guns be silent

fold hands on words

let the Normandy hills
read the poem
he has become

John Jarmain

Sketch of John Jarmain by
Evelyn Ethel Jarmain née Houghton

William John Fletcher Jarmain [or John Jarmain] was
born on February 4th, 1910, in Hertfordshire. He was
educated at Shrewsbury School in Shropshire, then
gained a degree in mathematics at Queens' College,
Cambridge. Before the war he taught English, math
and sometimes French and Italian at Millfield School
in Street, Somerset. Here he found time to write his
novel Priddy Barrows (Collins 1944) which is set in
Somerset with a Brontë-like atmosphere and a cast of
vivid characters.

His 1934 marriage to Evelyn gave him a son, Mark,
and a daughter, Joanna. The marriage ended in divorce
and John then married Beryl with whom he had two
daughters and a son.

A copy of *Alice in Wonderland*, Robert Browning's
poems, and Shakespeare's works accompanied John into
war for he was a great reader, also a bird-watcher with
a deep love for the English countryside. He wrote a
number of poems, some of them published in small war-
time magazines. He died on June 26, 1944.

Embarkation, 1942.

In undetected trains we left our land
At evening secretly from wayside stations.
None knew our place of parting; no pale hand
Waved as we went, not one friend said farewell.
But grouped on weedgrown platforms
Only a few officials holding watches
Noted the stealthy hour of our departing,
And, as we went, turned back to their hotel.

With blinds drawn down we left the things we know,
The simple fields, the homely ricks and yards;
Passed willows greyly bunching to the moon
And English towns. But in our blindfold train
Already these were far and long ago,
Stored quiet pictures which the mind must keep:
We saw them not. Instead we played at cards,
Or strangely dropped asleep.

Then in a callow dawn we stood in lines
Like foreigners on bare and unknown quays,
Till someone bravely into the hollow of waiting
Cast a timid wisp of song;
It moved along the lines of patient soldiers

P.T.O.

Soldiers' Prayer

We do not ask that fate shall mitigate
Whatever hardship we may have to bear.
Nor that we shall not suffer in our share,
Or more, whatever come of wounds and hate:
We do not ask for any recompense
Nor for remembrance in the triumph-day.
Our youth is wasted in its own defence;
Not all your laurels can restore to us
The years that are taken away
With every untouched promise that they bore.
Only we pray that when the guns cease fire
We may return, and not find all things changed.
That then in answer to our heart's desire
We find love waiting, that we feared estranged.

by John Jarmain, from *Poems*, Collins 1945. p.25

Left: Manuscript page for "Embarcation" from John
Jarmain's *Poems*.

Joanna M. Weston grew up on the North Downs of Kent, under one of the main bombing runs to London. She left England at aged 18 for Canada where she has lived ever since, becoming Canadian on February 15, 1965, the day the maple leaf flag was adopted. She is a full-time writer of poetry, short-stories, children's books and poetry reviews. She has published internationally in journals and anthologies and has two middle-readers, *The Willow-Tree Girl* and *Those Blue Shoes*, in print.